LIVING WITH
DISORDERS AND
DISABILITIES

LIVING WITH
PTSD

by Lindsay Wyskowski

ReferencePoint
Press®

San Diego, CA

For more information, contact:
ReferencePoint Press, Inc.
PO Box 27779
San Diego, CA 92198
www.ReferencePointPress.com

Content Consultant: Carmen P. McLean, PhD, Perelman School of Medicine, University
of Pennsylvania

LIBRARY OF CONGRESS CATALOGING-IN-PUBLICATION DATA

Name: Wyskowski, Lindsay, 1986– author.
Title: Living with PTSD / by Lindsay Wyskowski.
Description: San Diego, CA : ReferencePoint Press, Inc., [2019] | Series: Living with
    Disorders and Disabilities | Audience: Grade 9 to 12. Includes bibliographical references
    and index.
Identifiers: LCCN 2018011541 (print) | LCCN 2018011763 (ebook) | ISBN 9781682824900
    (ebook) | ISBN 9781682824894 (hardcover)
Subjects: LCSH: Post-traumatic stress disorder—Juvenile literature.
Classification: LCC RC552.P67 (ebook) | LCC RC552.P67 W97 2019 (print) | DDC
    616.85/21—dc23
LC record available at https://lccn.loc.gov/2018011541

CONTENTS

WEATHERING THE STORM OF PTSD

Ana had enjoyed living by the ocean all her life. She had heard about hurricanes before, learning about them during science class at school and seeing photos from storms that had made landfall in other places. Having never experienced hurricanes firsthand, she didn't worry about them too much.

That all changed when Ana was fifteen. A major hurricane blew through her city, knocking out power and flooding the streets. Ana and her family followed the recommendation of local authorities and evacuated from their home, but they almost didn't make it out of their neighborhood because of rising flood waters. The water that had started flowing into Ana's house swirled around their car as they drove away. When they returned home after the storm, everything about Ana's life was different than it had been before the storm. The flood waters had devastated Ana's home, along with other homes and businesses in her neighborhood. Ana looked around her ruined living room and felt overwhelmed when she remembered the way water

A person with PTSD often feels worried, afraid, or sad. These feelings persist long after the trauma itself has passed.

poured in from the flood. School was closed, so Ana spent all her time helping her family clean up the ruined belongings that littered the first floor of their home.

Even months after the storm, Ana felt uneasy. She had trouble sleeping, and her heart started to thump in her chest when the wind started to blow. Ana did not find joy in being near the ocean anymore. Her lungs felt like they were frozen when she passed the beach. Ana was experiencing panic attacks. She was constantly worried, afraid, and sad. The hurricane and its impact had traumatized Ana, and she felt unsafe in her longtime family home, even when every trace of the hurricane had been wiped away. Though her house was seemingly back in order, Ana could not help worrying that another hurricane would trap her inside her home in deep water.

Traumatic Natural Disasters

Ana is not a real girl, but her story illustrates the personal trauma that can be brought on by severe, unexpected weather. Hurricanes, tornadoes, and other catastrophic weather events can make a lasting impression on people living in the storms' paths. The storms' effects are not limited to the physical devastation that can result; more long-lasting effects come in the form of psychological trauma. Some people have great emotional difficulty processing such events and their aftermath. After living through such a life-changing event, it can be hard not to live in fear that such a terrible event will happen again.

Ermence Parent survived a major weather event in 2005 when Hurricane Katrina hit New Orleans, Louisiana. More than a decade after having her home swamped by 8 feet (2.4 m) of water, she still experiences psychological distress associated with that traumatic event. "The problem with mental health issues is they don't go away," she said. "You can try to bury them if you like, but they only get worse."[1]

Parent was not alone in struggling with the trauma brought on by Hurricane Katrina. It was a massive

"The problem with mental health issues is they don't go away. You can try to bury them if you like, but they only get worse."[1]

—Ermence Parent,
Hurricane Katrina survivor

Natural disasters such as hurricanes cause psychological trauma along with physical devastation. People who lose their homes often suffer from anxiety, depression, and PTSD.

storm, pummeling New Orleans and the surrounding area. Thousands of people lost their homes, and almost two thousand people lost their lives. Tyffani Delacruz also lived through Katrina. The storm hit Tyffani's New Orleans home when she was thirteen years old. Her family evacuated, and they lost their home to the flooding. "All of a sudden, we were homeless," Tyffani said. "I come from a nice, middle-class family. You never think at 13 that everything can be taken away from you, but that's what happened."[2]

Tyffani's reaction to the trauma manifested itself in the form of depression. When her family had to relocate outside of New Orleans, she was treated badly for being homeless. "A lot of people were calling us refugees and treating us poorly," she said, "like we were beneath them because they knew that we didn't have anything." Tyffani experienced the stress of having everything but her family taken away from her. "I was mad," she said. "Things were never the same again after that. . . . Nothing was ever consistent again in my life."[3]

Hurricanes are not the only natural disasters that can have devastating consequences for those who live through them. Earthquakes, tornadoes, and wildfires can also be traumatic, especially when the damage affects whole communities. Judith Floyd lived through a wildfire in Gatlinburg, Tennessee, and she explains how she felt after the fires were extinguished: "You get very scared. You get depressed. You get panicky and have high anxiety. I'm very shaky all the time. . . . I'm always afraid I'm going to come back to my house burned to the ground. I'm neurotic about unplugging things. It's turned me into a very paranoid person."[4]

Trauma Affects Mental Health

Natural disasters are just one event that may cause deep psychological trauma. Motor vehicle accidents, terrorist attacks, assault, life-threatening illnesses, the sudden death of a loved one, and abuse can all be traumatic. Trauma is hard to process, and survivors of traumatic events can experience an array of symptoms sometimes classified as a mental health condition called post-traumatic stress disorder, or PTSD. PTSD symptoms can make it difficult for a person to work, attend school, maintain healthy relationships, or participate in everyday life. Having a severe reaction to trauma is not out of the ordinary, says Louisiana coroner Charles Preston. Preston lived through Hurricane Katrina and witnessed the emotional havoc it wreaked. "Hyper vigilance, excessive fear or anxiety, denial, bursts of rage and even self-isolation can all be symptoms of PTSD. If you're feeling it, that's OK. It's normal."[5]

"Hyper vigilance, excessive fear or anxiety, denial, bursts of rage and even self-isolation can all be symptoms of PTSD. If you're feeling it, that's OK. It's normal."[5]

— *Charles Preston, coroner in Louisiana*

Even when people live through something terrible, they may not be aware that they have PTSD. Abuse survivor Dani Bostick writes, "When I figured out I had PTSD, I was surprised. I thought I was doing really well for years and years. In hindsight, I was just numb and had a constricted range of feelings, also related to the trauma."[6] Learning more about the nature and scope of PTSD can help those who are affected get the help they need to lead productive lives.

Chapter 1

WHAT IS PTSD?

The world is full of uncertainty, and unexpected events and experiences often bring unwelcome consequences. In some cases, these experiences can have a lifelong effect on a person's overall well-being. Severe traumatic events—such as a bombing, a mass shooting, or the death of a loved one—can bring on panic, depression, rage, and anxiety. A person who experiences such emotions for long periods of time is typically diagnosed with PTSD.

PTSD is something that can develop in people after traumatic experiences, whether they were one-time occurrences or experiences happening over time. The word *post* in the name of this condition signifies that the debilitating effects arise after a traumatic situation. According to the Anxiety and Depression Association of America, "PTSD is a serious potentially debilitating condition that can occur in people who have experienced or witnessed a natural disaster, serious accident, terrorist incident, sudden death of a loved one, war, violent personal assault such as rape, or other life-threatening events."[7]

Unexpected events happen every day that could cause someone to be traumatized.

Not everyone who has a traumatic life experience will be diagnosed with PTSD. In fact, the National Center for PTSD indicates that "about 7 or 8 out of every 100 people . . . will have PTSD at some point in their lives."[8] In any given year, approximately 8 million adults in the United States are living with PTSD.

> "About 7 or 8 out of every 100 people . . . will have PTSD at some point in their lives."[8]
>
> —*National Center for PTSD*

PTSD in Children

PTSD can affect children as well as adults. Children can develop PTSD based on how severe an incident is, how close they are to the incident, and how their parents or caregivers react. Sometimes medical procedures a child receives before he or she is even old enough to walk or talk can cause symptoms of PTSD later in life. If a traumatic event happens near a child or to someone the child knows, the child is at risk of developing PTSD just as if he or she had experienced the event firsthand. PTSD is sometimes caused not by a single incident but by chronic abuse or neglect. All too often, this abuse is committed by parents or other caregivers who fail in their most basic responsibility to protect a child's welfare.

PTSD in children is not studied as widely as it is in adults, so it is difficult to determine exactly how many children are affected by the condition. Sometimes PTSD is undiagnosed for a long time after either a singular incident or chronic abuse. "Parents may not spot the signs of PTSD for the same reasons that parents may miss many mental

It can be difficult to diagnose PTSD in children if they can't describe their feelings. Trained psychologists must learn to spot the disorder's signs.

health difficulties, particularly emotional disorders like anxiety and depression," said Richard Meiser-Stedman, a physician in England. "Poor mental health may often be a very private experience, and children find it difficult to describe their thoughts and feelings."[9] Still, according to the studies performed so far, the National Institute of Mental Health (NIMH) estimates that nearly 7 percent of girls and approximately 2 percent of boys who experience a traumatic event develop PTSD.

Trauma, Grief, and PTSD

Traumatic events can happen to an individual person or to many people at once. Sometimes people will feel deeply traumatized when someone they love has an accident or a serious illness. Parents sometimes develop PTSD when their children are fighting cancer. "As parents, we want our kids to be safe," said psychologist Nancy Kassam-Adams. "Once you've been through this, you know they will never be 100 percent safe, and it's hard to stop thinking about it."[10] Overwhelming, recurring feelings of worry and fear are associated with PTSD.

> "Poor mental health may often be a very private experience, and children find it difficult to describe their thoughts and feelings."[9]
>
> —Richard Meiser-Stedman, British physician

After experiencing something traumatic, people may try to cope in a variety of ways. Coping mechanisms differ from person to person. When someone is trying to process how they feel after a traumatic event, it is not uncommon to feel upset and scared, dwell on what happened, and be unable to sleep or concentrate. Traumatic events can cause people to lose their appetite, be numb to the world around them, or even feel nothing at all. These reactions are common for survivors of traumatic events and are symptoms of PTSD. NIMH states that "for most people, these are normal and expected responses and generally lessen with time."[11]

These same responses may occur in people engaged in the grieving process. Grief and PTSD are different, but they share similar characteristics. PTSD can result from a variety of situations and experiences, but the grieving process is more specific. Grief is what people experience when they lose something or someone close to them. Examples include the death of a spouse or family member, the end of a close relationship, or the loss of a beloved pet.

Psychiatry professor Katherine Shear explains grief as "the form that love takes after someone you love dies. The point isn't to put these feelings behind you altogether; that's not possible or even desirable. The point is to gain perspective and help grief find its rightful place in a person's life."[12] Grieving is a natural way to deal with loss, and everyone has to find his or her own way of dealing with the pain.

When someone is grieving, the body and mind can react in a variety of ways. Some responses are physical in nature, such as shortness of breath or extreme fatigue. Emotions can be intense and wide-ranging, including feeling sad, scared, anxious, angry, or guilty. A grieving person may want to be alone to a great extent. These responses are also common in a person with PTSD. With both grief and PTSD, a person may have angry outbursts and a feeling of detachment or separation from the world. In both cases, the person might try to avoid reminders of the loved one who died or the traumatic event that brought on PTSD. He or she may lose interest in activities or hobbies that were once greatly enjoyed.

While grief usually subsides over time, there can be instances when grief reactions don't go away. This can mean someone has a mental health disorder called prolonged grief disorder, or complicated grief. In both prolonged grief and PTSD, symptoms do not subside over time and are usually present for long periods—even years after a triggering incident occurred. Because of its extended duration, PTSD is typically considered to be chronic in nature. A less common

Both grief and PTSD can cause physical as well as emotional responses to loss. The aftereffects can impact a person's daily life for a long time.

version of PTSD is known as delayed PTSD, meaning symptoms do not emerge until six months or more after a triggering incident. Delayed PTSD is rare, and it most commonly occurs in adults who experienced trauma as children. Regardless of when people start exhibiting signs of PTSD, the condition can interrupt their normal routines and their relationships with family and friends.

Additionally, while anyone can experience grief, PTSD is identified by a more specific set of clinical criteria outlined by the American Psychiatric Association (APA). The APA has included PTSD in its *Diagnostic and Statistical Manual of Mental Disorders* since 1980, and people must exhibit multiple symptoms in order to receive this diagnosis from a mental health professional.

Who Is Diagnosed with PTSD?

PTSD can affect anyone. Because people are so different, PTSD will look different for everyone who is battling the condition. No two people will experience PTSD in the same way, even if their trauma is very similar or from the same event. Some people are more likely to develop PTSD than others. The disparity can be based on age or gender. Adults ages forty to sixty are usually at a greater risk of developing PTSD than older or younger people, as are women in general. The National Center for PTSD reports that "women are more than twice as likely to develop PTSD than men (10% for women and 4% for men)."[13] Part of the reason more women develop PTSD is that they are more likely to experience sexual assault, a common cause of PTSD. Researchers are currently studying the potential link between genetics and risk of PTSD.

Another common factor among PTSD sufferers of all ages is that often the survivors had experienced trauma at some point previously in their lives. Joseph Boscarino has studied PTSD for thirty years. He assessed the mental health status of residents of Monmouth County, New Jersey, after the devastation caused by Hurricane Sandy in 2012. He noted, "Usually people who get the disorder have had other issues before the exposure, and this can bring it out. Also, if they had health issues and financial problems, it impacts it as well. [The] storm is the last cable that snaps."[14]

Sometimes traumatic incidents occur in a place a person thought was safe, such as school, home, or one's neighborhood. Helaina Hovitz had just started seventh grade when planes hit the World Trade Center in New York City as part of a terrorist attack on

Far-reaching traumatic events such as the terrorist attacks of September 11, 2001, cause a terrible physical toll. They can also cause PTSD in many people at once.

September 11, 2001. Her school and the apartment building where she lived were close to the disaster, and everyone was on edge for weeks that another attack was coming. Even after normalcy returned to Helaina's neighborhood, she was still stricken with fear:

> I wasn't sleeping. I was always worried, paranoid, ready to take off at the next attack, having nightmares and flashbacks, feeling like a sitting duck waiting to die. While the rest of the world resumed "normalcy," it became very clear to me that because of what was happening in my brain and my body, and what

> "I wasn't sleeping. I was always worried, paranoid, ready to take off at the next attack, having nightmares and flashbacks, feeling like a sitting duck waiting to die. While the rest of the world resumed 'normalcy,' it became very clear to me that because of what was happening in my brain and my body, and what continued to happen outside of my front door, nothing would ever feel normal again."[15]
>
> —Helaina Hovitz, 9/11 trauma survivor

continued to happen outside of my front door, nothing would ever feel normal again.[15]

Once Helaina shared her troubling feelings with her parents, she saw a series of therapists over the course of years who misdiagnosed her condition. It was only when she met with a therapist who recognized her symptoms as being consistent with PTSD and she received appropriate treatment that she started to improve.

Military Origins

Not surprisingly, war veterans are frequently diagnosed with PTSD after they engage in active combat. Historical records suggest troops experienced PTSD during the Civil War (1861–1865), though the condition was not called PTSD at the time. After the Civil War, family members of returning troops noticed the men had changed, but they weren't sure what had happened. Doctors believed something was affecting soldiers' cardiovascular systems—blood pressure, pulse, and heart—so the behavioral and emotional changes were dubbed "Soldier's Heart." The treatments service members received in those days, such as bed rest and sedatives, were mostly ineffective.

During World War I (1914–1918), PTSD was often referred to as "shell shock" because of troops' prolonged exposure to artillery fire. Physicians believed the explosion of artillery shells caused brain damage and a host of physical manifestations. Researchers were puzzled when, early in the war, British troops who had not sustained any physical injuries began exhibiting symptoms such as dizziness, headaches, debilitating anxiety, facial tics, nightmares, and diarrhea. In fact, in 1917, while the war was still underway, one-seventh of the British army's disability discharges were because of "war neuroses." During World War II (1939–1945), the favored term for the condition now known as PTSD was Combat Stress Reaction (CSR), also known as "battle fatigue." Some military leaders, such as US general George S. Patton, did not believe battle fatigue was a real syndrome. The main goal of treatment was to return troops to the battlefield. Combat veterans often chose not to discuss what they had seen in combat unless they were talking to another serviceman. Typically veterans kept their war stories and their feelings to themselves, often bearing substantial emotional pain.

In part because of research involving returning veterans of the Vietnam War (1954–1975), the APA coined the term *post-traumatic stress disorder* in 1980. The condition was listed in the *Diagnostic and Statistical Manual of Mental Disorders* for the first time in that year.

While people of every age and occupation can be diagnosed with PTSD, members of the military experience PTSD at a higher rate than the general population. Researchers have tracked how many troops have been diagnosed with PTSD from the Vietnam War through the

Members of the military are at particular risk of developing PTSD. They face traumatic events, such as firefights and explosions, as part of their duty.

wars of the 2000s. Roughly 30 percent of all troops who served in Vietnam have experienced PTSD in their lifetime. More recently, approximately 12 percent of veterans of the Gulf War (1990–1991) have PTSD in a given year, compared to 11 to 20 percent of veterans of the wars in Iraq and Afghanistan in the early 2000s. Both women and men who have served in the armed forces are at risk for PTSD because of experiences they have had on the battlefield and during their service in general. With the widespread use of improvised explosive devices (IEDs) by enemy combatants in the Middle East, even non-battle situations can bring traumatic consequences for service personnel.

Service members injured in combat may focus on their external injuries, not realizing they have been mentally injured as well. Dexter Pitts served in Iraq, where he was injured by a bomb. While recovering from that injury, an incident occurred that made him realize his injuries were not limited to what the eye could see. When his cousin kept making noise and bothering him, he snapped. He said, "I just lost it. I blacked out. I chased him down the hallway, grabbed him by his shirt, picked him up and punched him in his chest as hard as I could."[16]

Just as veterans themselves may be unaware of the psychological injuries they sustained in combat, friends and family members may also fail to see the internal wounds that compromise veterans' emotional well-being. Joseph Hammond, a Vietnam veteran, said, "A lot of people, they don't see a wound on the outside. So [they say] how can there be something wrong with you? But they don't understand the mental part of it. There's memories. There's things that you've seen over there that you don't want to discuss with anybody."[17]

Even service members who do not sustain physical or psychological injuries when deployed can find it difficult to return to their normal, everyday lives. While they may enjoy returning to their family, they often miss the companionship of fellow service members with whom they shared so much.

Sebastian Junger understands the difficulties of adjusting to civilian life. Junger's PTSD set in after he returned home from Afghanistan.

> "A lot of people, they don't see a wound on the outside. So [they say] how can there be something wrong with you? But they don't understand the mental part of it. There's memories. There's things that you've seen over there that you don't want to discuss with anybody."[17]
>
> —Joseph Hammond, Vietnam veteran

Junger explains,

I mentally buried all of it until one day, a few months later, when I went into the subway at rush hour to catch the C train downtown. Suddenly I found myself backed up against a metal support column, absolutely convinced I was going to die. There were too many people on the platform, the trains were coming into the station too fast, the lights were too bright, the world was too loud. I couldn't quite explain what was wrong, but I was far more scared than I'd ever been in Afghanistan.[18]

After experiencing several more panic attacks in confined, crowded places, Junger's symptoms gradually went away. Only later did a psychotherapist identify them as having been caused by PTSD. While there is no cure for PTSD, symptoms can often be eliminated to the point of remission with proper treatment. Early and effective treatment can improve the lives of PTSD survivors in the long run.

Secondary PTSD

Unlike infectious diseases, PTSD does not readily spread from one person to another. However, there is some evidence that secondary PTSD exists, where people who are repeatedly exposed to the details of trauma or symptoms of others living with PTSD can start exhibiting symptoms of the disorder, too.

For example, a New York City psychologist named Michael (last name withheld) treated hundreds of people who were affected by the September 11, 2001, attacks on the World Trade Center. Day after day, he heard stories about the trauma his patients experienced during and after the attacks. By 2004, he was having panic attacks, was anxious and depressed, and was unable to sleep most nights. He came to

School Shootings and PTSD

When gun violence occurs in a school, students and teachers can suffer lasting effects, especially since school has traditionally been considered a safe place. In 1999, two students at Columbine High School in Littleton, Colorado, murdered twelve students and one teacher, wounding twenty-three others. Kent Friesen taught chemistry at Columbine at the time. Ten years after the shooting, he still experienced physical illness and emotional outbursts in relation to the shooting. "Post-traumatic stress can happen to anybody. It's mind-boggling to know that people still don't believe in it. It's real, and it's one of those things that just won't go away unless you get help," he said.[1]

Experiencing gun violence at school means children sometimes lose their sense of security. First-grader Siena Kibilko lost a classmate and close friend during a shooting at her South Carolina school. After the incident, she avoided going places she once loved. For example, she did not want to attend summer camp. "They don't have a police officer," she told her mother.[2]

While these events can be scary and life-changing, it is important to know that support from friends, families, and trained therapists can ease the symptoms of PTSD. Therapy and support groups can help survivors start to feel safe again.

1. Susan Donaldson James, "Columbine Shootings 10 Years Later: Students, Teacher Still Haunted by Post-Traumatic Stress," *ABC News*, April 13, 2009. abcnews.go.com.

2. John Woodrow Cox, "Twelve Seconds of Gunfire," *Washington Post*, June 9, 2017, www.washingtonpost.com.

realize he likely had a form of PTSD because of his exposure to the stories he internalized over time. "I felt my health eroding, but I could only diagnose it in hindsight," he said. "I didn't realize the full extent of what was happening."[19] He stopped working as a therapist for a while so he could control his own symptoms, later returning to his practice to help others deal with trauma.

People can develop PTSD through exposure to the details of traumatic events, as Michael did, and they can also develop mental health problems because of the stress that comes from living with a loved one who has PTSD. This is why family members of veterans, especially spouses or partners, are at a higher risk for developing secondary PTSD. Veteran Caleb Vines shows signs of severe PTSD after having been deployed to Iraq twice. He has terrifying nightmares, is unable to work, and occasionally starts yelling when he is out in public places. Brannan, Caleb's wife and primary caregiver, is sometimes unable to do tasks because of her emotional state, showing signs of PTSD even though she has never been to war. She says, "Sometimes I can't do the laundry. And it's not like, 'Oh, I'm too tired to do the laundry,' it's like, 'Um, I don't understand how to turn the washing machine on.' I am looking at a washing machine and a pile of laundry and my brain is literally overwhelmed by trying to figure out how to reconcile them."[20]

Children can also show signs of PTSD when a parent exhibits PTSD symptoms. The Vines's young daughter, Katie (a pseudonym), acts out at school, has angry outbursts toward other students, and anxiously picks at her skin. Brannan says, "She just mirrors" her dad's behavior. Katie, she says, is not "a normal, carefree six-year-old."[21]

Even if family members do not exhibit PTSD-like symptoms, they can be significantly affected by the PTSD of their loved one. Spouses such as Brannan Vines wear down under the stress of providing around-the-clock care for their spouse, overseeing the services and paperwork related to their spouse's care, managing a household, raising children in a difficult home environment, and perhaps holding an outside job. They do all of this while grieving the loss of emotional support they once had from their spouse.

Research confirms the challenges PTSD presents for family relationships. According to the National Center for PTSD, PTSD

The Resilience Factor

Certain factors make people more likely to be resilient when trauma occurs. Researchers are studying whether resilience is a learned quality or if it is something people are born with. In some cases, they have found resilience can be taught. "Resilience is common and can be witnessed all around us," says Steven M. Southwick, an expert on the effects of trauma. "Everyone can learn and train to be more resilient. The key involves knowing how to harness stress and use it to our advantage."[1]

One example of resilience can be found in US Air Force veteran and 1936 Olympian Louis Zamperini. Zamperini lived through a harrowing series of events during World War II. First, his plane was shot down, trapping him and two airmen on a life raft in the ocean for forty-seven days until they were picked up by a Japanese patrol boat. For the next two years, Zamperini was treated brutally as a prisoner of war. After the war, Zamperini dealt with depression, nightmares, and alcohol abuse, but he went on to become a motivational speaker, preaching forgiveness.

"Zamperini was defiant, a risk-taker . . . people who are like that, people who are optimists, tend to be more resilient, and there's a genetic component in those traits," says Southwick.[2] People with a strong support system who are confident in their own ability to cope with stressful situations and channel the power of positive thinking tend to be more resilient in the face of a traumatic event.

1. Steven M. Southwick, "The Science of Resilience," *Huffpost,* November 13, 2012. www.huffingtonpost.com.

2. David Cox, "Unbroken: What Makes Some People More Resilient Than Others?" *The Guardian,* December 19, 2014. www.theguardian.com.

causes "severe and pervasive negative effects on marital adjustment, general family functioning, and the mental health of partners. These negative effects result in such problems as compromised parenting, family violence, divorce, sexual problems, aggression, and caregiver burden."[22] Fortunately for PTSD sufferers, increased awareness about PTSD's far-reaching effects is making a difference. Services and support programs for PTSD victims and their families continue to expand over time.

Chapter 2

PTSD SYMPTOMS AND DIAGNOSIS

Anyone who experiences trauma, whether during one event or over a period of time, is at risk for developing PTSD. The symptoms of PTSD can vary from person to person, and PTSD symptoms are not always visible to the naked eye. Because these symptoms aren't always obvious and because it may take months or years for them to appear, it is essential that people experiencing such symptoms be treated by skilled medical practitioners.

Erica Jones (not her real name) has PTSD from her time serving in the military. Jones was injured when a bomb exploded near her. Two of the friends she served with were so stricken by their wartime experiences that they committed suicide to escape their anguish. It took Jones six years to get help for her condition because she didn't feel she deserved it compared to what her friends had gone through.

"A lot of my life is smoke and mirrors," Jones said. "On the outside, I look and act totally fine but on the inside, I'm a wreck. I still have sleepless nights and night terrors. I'm constantly paranoid, and I'm easily triggered by normal everyday things. The worst part is remembering my friends I lost to suicide."[23]

> "On the outside, I look and act totally fine but on the inside, I'm a wreck. I still have sleepless nights and night terrors. I'm constantly paranoid, and I'm easily triggered by normal everyday things."[23]
>
> —Erica Jones (pseudonym), military veteran

When the symptoms of PTSD set in, it might not be immediately evident that PTSD is the appropriate diagnosis. C. David Moody Jr. was abused as a child, and he hid his trauma for many years. Then one day more than twenty years after the abusive incidents, Moody was driving to the gym and had a panic attack. He didn't realize that what he was experiencing was related to the trauma he sustained earlier in his life. "The first thing I did was [to get] a bunch of tests because I thought I had a brain tumor or something," he says. "When I first started having panic attacks, I thought I was losing my mind. People are always telling you, 'It's just in your head, let it go,' but it's not that easy."[24]

To understand what PTSD looks like, it's important to understand how the symptoms work together to alter someone's life. Symptoms from PTSD are grouped into four categories: intrusive

Managing stress and anger appropriately can be one of the many challenges facing a person with PTSD. Sufferers may have outbursts against their friends or family.

memories or re-experiencing the event, avoidance, negative changes in thinking patterns and mood, and changes in physical and emotional reactions. Symptoms may not be constant, and they may start soon after a traumatic event or not appear until months or years afterward. According to current clinical standards, in order to be diagnosed with PTSD, a person must have all of the following symptoms for at least one month:

- At least one re-experiencing symptom (such as flashbacks or nightmares).

- At least one avoidance symptom (such as avoiding thoughts or places that bring back bad memories).

- At least two cognition and mood symptoms (such as having trouble remembering the trauma, negative or suicidal thoughts, or diminished interest in previously enjoyable activities).

- At least two arousal and reactivity symptoms (such as being tense or easily startled, having trouble sleeping, or lashing out in anger).

Re-experiencing Trauma

For people living with PTSD, intrusive memories can be one of the more challenging symptoms to overcome, in part because they return unpredictably. Seth Gillihan, who researches PTSD, says, "Part of the haunting quality of PTSD is that these memories live with us. The memory can come up uninvited without any obvious triggers and these memories will just run through as your mind tries to process and make sense of them."[25]

Everyone has memories. Memories are what allow people to have conversations, remember email addresses, and write sentences. A memory can be as simple as what a person ate for lunch last week or a conversation with a fellow passenger on the bus. Memories help people navigate through each day. These are not the types of memories referred to when discussing intrusive memories. Intrusive memories are rooted in the trauma people experience and

> "Part of the haunting quality of PTSD is that these memories live with us. The memory can come up uninvited without any obvious triggers and these memories will just run through as your mind tries to process and make sense of them."[25]
>
> —Seth Gillihan, PTSD researcher

are controlled by the way the brain processes the recollection of a traumatic event or series of events.

For the average person who does not have PTSD, when something momentous happens, the associated memory is referred to as a "flashbulb memory." In such cases, people attach an emotional connection to the memory and can vividly recall what happened, even much later. This is common with catastrophic events such as the attacks that took place on September 11, 2001. Memories like these, which are typically not personally traumatic, tend to fade over time. One study surveyed 200 people about the details of the September 11 attacks ten days after they occurred. These people were not closely affected by the tragedy. One year later, there were major inconsistencies in how they remembered the event when compared to their initial answers. Only about two-thirds of their recollections were correct.

As unsettling as memories can be for the majority of the population, memories can be even more disturbing for someone with PTSD. This is because certain aspects of a traumatic event tend to be remembered at unexpected times. These intrusive memories can be triggered by a variety of factors, including weather conditions, sounds, smells, emotions, or people connected with the original trauma. A PTSD survivor's brain reacts to triggering stimuli that were present when the trauma occurred even though that person faces no real danger at the moment. Normally, the portion of the brain known as the hippocampus manages memory functions, much like a mental filing cabinet. In PTSD survivors, however, the amygdala portion of the brain, which controls strong emotions such as fear, assumes a more prominent role than it did previously. An overactive amygdala

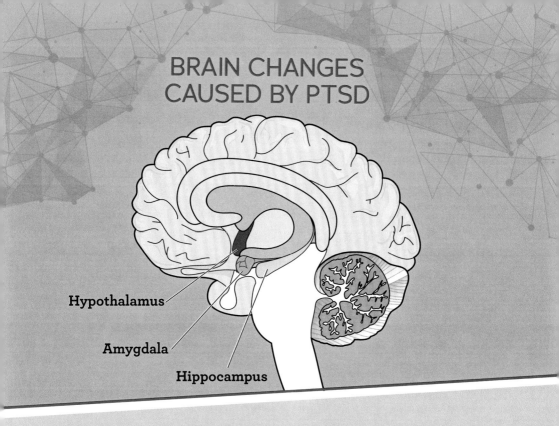

BRAIN CHANGES CAUSED BY PTSD

Hypothalamus

Amygdala

Hippocampus

The hippocampus is normally responsible for managing memory and regulating emotions. In people with PTSD, the amygdala becomes overactive relative to the hippocampus, prompting a rise in anxiety and fear.

produces an autonomic fight-or-flight response to certain stimuli. Triggers that present reminders of trauma can bring back intrusive, distressing memories that are isolated from a person's normal memory. These recollections can sometimes be accompanied by pronounced physical reactions such as sweating, rapid breathing, or a racing heart.

Nightmares are also common for a person with PTSD. Nightmares may or may not depict the traumatic event someone experienced. "Nightmares . . . can be like a movie, or they can even be weird dreams in which the event you witnessed gets morphed in certain ways," says Charles Marmar, a psychiatrist and director of the PTSD research program at New York University's Langone Medical Center.[26] The story taking place within a nightmare can be so distressing to the person dreaming that it prompts a physical reaction, such as punching or choking someone who is nearby.

Flashbacks, in contrast, happen when people are awake. During a flashback, people are so immersed in experiencing a memory that they lose touch with their present surroundings. "I've been lucky not to experience nightmares, but I can't say the same for my waking hours. I can't tell you how many times I've [relived] the past in my head," said Melissa Wilson, who is living with PTSD after years of bullying.[27] Flashbacks can be a very unsettling experience for someone who experienced trauma. They can last anywhere from a few minutes to hours or days.

Sexual assault victim Monika Sudakov has PTSD and emphasizes that her flashbacks are not like the enjoyable memories other people have of family vacations or special moments. She writes, "For most people, myself included, flashbacks are an intense re-experience of a traumatic event, which feels like it's happening now and involves all your senses. In effect, it feels like being re-traumatized, even though you are not actually experiencing the event for real."[28] As with intrusive

"For most people, myself included, flashbacks are an intense re-experience of a traumatic event, which feels like it's happening now and involves all your senses. In effect, it feels like being re-traumatized, even though you are not actually experiencing the event for real."[28]

—Monika Sudakov, sexual assault victim

memories, flashbacks can be brought on by certain smells, sounds, and sights that serve as reminders of the traumatic incident or events that caused the onset of PTSD. People who have flashbacks might feel a physical sensation, such as pain or pressure, and they might also experience the same emotions they felt when the triggering event occurred. Fortunately for those living with PTSD, flashbacks tend to be less common than nightmares.

Avoidance

It is common for people with PTSD to avoid anything that might remind them of the traumatic event from their past. They often try not to think or talk about the trauma they lived through, and they also may stay away from people, places, or things that bring up thoughts and feelings about what happened. They also may be unable to remember significant details about their trauma. "Avoidance is the glue that holds PTSD together, as it perpetuates negative assumptions and eventually shrinks one's world down over time," says psychologist Vanessa H. Roddenberry.[29] Someone who has PTSD as a result of a car accident, for example, might quit driving because she is worried about being involved in another accident. Another person might withdraw from friends with whom he served in the military for fear that uncomfortable topics will be brought up when they get together.

People with PTSD employ many strategies to avoid facing their trauma. Some may keep so busy they don't have time to think about their emotional discomfort. Others shut down their feelings, becoming numb to their thoughts or even to their own bodies. Still others turn to drugs or alcohol as a way to escape. It is not uncommon for a PTSD survivor to adopt a pessimistic attitude about the future, believing that he or she will die young or that there is no purpose in living. Poor life choices can result for those who believe their lives are pointless and are certain to end soon.

But Patricia Resick, professor of psychiatry and behavioral sciences at Duke University, says avoiding reminders of trauma can backfire. "If you try to bury it and not think about it, it can smack you in the face," she says.[30] People who try to avoid certain places or topics might be caught off guard when they are suddenly exposed to something that reminds them of their own experience. A woman who was assaulted, for example, might experience great distress just by hearing a news story about a situation similar to her own. While avoidance may be a necessary coping strategy at certain points in one's recovery, it is not seen as the most helpful long-term approach.

Negative Changes in Thinking and Mood

PTSD can impact how people are feeling about themselves and the world around them. Someone with PTSD might develop thoughts that make regular, everyday tasks impossible because the negative thoughts are so overwhelming. After Jordan Rivkin's father committed suicide, Rivkin thought he had dealt with the loss. But after two years, his body was telling him otherwise. He consulted doctors, thinking something was wrong with his brain. "Not long after, everything fell apart," Rivkin said, "I had no idea why, but my best guess was that either I was going crazy or dying. I quit work. I withdrew from university. And I retreated to bed, gripped by fear."[31]

Rivkin could not carry out the simplest of tasks, and for six months he was able to function only with the help of medication. "All the while, the world looked different," he said. "It didn't seem as real as it once had, and my head felt lost in a fog, like I wasn't part of my surroundings. I felt like I was slipping away, and thought of death often during that time. I welcomed danger, and recall riding my bike and wishing a truck would hit me and put an end to my misery."[32]

People with PTSD often have negative thoughts about themselves and think their loved ones would be better off without them. They may feel guilt or shame about what happened to them, sometimes even blaming themselves for what occurred. Their unfavorable view of themselves causes them to pull back from friends and family, and those relationships can suffer as a result. PTSD sufferers may lose hope in the future and have trouble staying involved and invested in activities they once enjoyed. Their illness can cause them to feel disconnected and unsafe, and powerful feelings such as anger, fear, and guilt can cloud their view of what is happening around them. And, when they are in the grips of so much negative emotion, they may be unable to tap into counterbalancing positive emotions, such as happiness or love.

Sometimes people are not sure they have PTSD because their symptoms may be attributed to other, more common disorders such as depression, anxiety, and obsessive-compulsive disorder.

> "All the while, the world looked different. It didn't seem as real as it once had, and my head felt lost in a fog, like I wasn't part of my surroundings. I felt like I was slipping away, and thought of death often during that time."[32]
>
> —Jordan Rivkin, PTSD sufferer after father's suicide

Obtaining an accurate diagnosis is critical in developing an effective treatment plan.

Changes in Physical and Emotional Reactions

Changes to the way a person responds and acts in various situations are a classic sign of PTSD. A soldier returning from war might be easily frightened when someone surprises her, putting her on high alert for the danger her brain tells her might be nearby. Because people with PTSD are often on edge, they typically have a hard time sleeping or concentrating. They might also be irritable, angry, or aggressive toward others.

Another way people with PTSD reveal their emotional turmoil is to act completely out of character. A person might uncharacteristically take part in dangerous or self-destructive behaviors, such as driving too fast or drinking excessively. Sometimes risky or self-harming behaviors appear long after trauma took place. When people experience trauma as children, they are more likely to smoke or abuse alcohol and other substances later on. They are also at greater risk for obesity and other serious illnesses as they age. Other long-lasting impacts include the tendency to self-harm, such as head banging, cutting, burning, and other forms of self-mutilation. One study found that among people who self-harmed on a regular basis, more than 90 percent were victims of sexual abuse. Thoughts of suicide and specific plans to commit suicide are also more common among people with PTSD than among the population as a whole. In a study of residents affected by Hurricane Katrina, conducted one year after the storm, 5 percent of respondents had plans to commit suicide

PTSD Warning Signs

After trauma happens, there's no sure way to know if PTSD will set in. But certain warning signs warrant getting help from a professional. According to NIMH, warning signs to look for include:

- Worrying a lot or feeling very anxious, sad, or fearful
- Crying often
- Having trouble thinking clearly
- Having frightening thoughts; reliving the experience
- Feeling angry
- Having nightmares or difficulty sleeping
- Avoiding places or people that bring back disturbing memories and responses
- Headaches
- Stomach pain and digestive issues
- Feeling tired
- Racing heart and sweating
- Being very jumpy and easily startled

compared to only 1 percent of the same respondents four to seven months prior.

PTSD Symptoms in Children

While children may exhibit the same PTSD symptoms as adults, they may also present with age-related symptoms. Children who are younger than six years old, for example, may unwittingly display their distress by wetting the bed. Traumatic events might also cause young children to cry a lot, exhibit separation anxiety, act younger than their current age, or become less talkative with parents or adults they trust. Preverbal children might express their hurts through play. "Since they don't yet have a language, stress will be reflected in their mood, nightmares or even play time," says psychologist Gabriela Hernández Heimper.[33] A child might reenact the traumatic event while she is playing because she does not have a better way to express what she experienced.

School-aged children might not have flashbacks about traumatic moments the way adults do, but when they remember what happened, they might become confused about the order of events. This means children sometimes change the timeline of when or how the traumatic event occurred. According to the National Center for PTSD, children might also think there were signs that indicated the trauma was about to unfold. They will then be hypervigilant in watching for these signs again, trying to prevent another traumatic event from happening.

The symptoms of PTSD in teenagers are fairly similar to those that adults experience. There might be noticeable changes in their behavior and how they treat the people around them. Liz Campbell, who specializes in treating children and young adults, says, "A teenager might start engaging in risk-taking behaviors or blowing off school."[34] In addition to risky behaviors and skipping school, older children and teenagers might become more disrespectful to others or more disruptive. If their trauma is associated with someone close to them getting injured or dying, they might feel guilt over not protecting that person or vengeful toward whoever caused the person pain.

No matter the age of children potentially impacted by trauma, it is important to watch for changes in the way children react to the world around them. "Don't ignore the warning signs," says Asim Shah, director of the mood disorder research program at Ben Taub Hospital

PTSD and Chronic Pain

Studies show people who have PTSD may be more susceptible to chronic pain. Chronic pain is pain that lasts longer than a normal healing time. In the past, clinicians assumed chronic pain was attributable to injuries from surgery or accidents, headaches, arthritis, or other physical issues. New studies indicate stress and emotional trauma can also contribute to chronic pain. When people are stressed or anxious, they subconsciously tense their muscles. The muscles become fatigued more quickly and don't work as well as they should. Studies also show people who are living with a combination of chronic pain and PTSD often have more pain and a lower quality of life than people who have chronic pain but do not have PTSD.

The other side of the chronic pain–PTSD interaction is that people who have chronic pain may develop PTSD symptoms because of the burden of living with pain every day. According to the National Center for PTSD, approximately 15 to 35 percent of patients with chronic pain also have PTSD. Rachel Meeks, a chronic pain sufferer, realized she had PTSD because of how she reacts to doctors and treatment. "Why does calling a doctor put me in the throes of depression? . . . Perhaps my brain is perceiving doctors and hospitals as threats," she said. "If I was a wild animal human, these are the kind of instincts that would tell me to run from a volcano or fight off a bear. . . . My 'fight or flight' reactions in my brain are causing stress." For people whose chronic pain originated with a traumatic event, the pain itself can be a reminder of the original event, thus worsening their PTSD.

Rachel Meeks, "Chronic Illness and Post-Traumatic Stress Disorder," *Do I Look Sick?* (blog), April 4, 2014. doilooksick.com.

in Houston, Texas. Indicators to look for include "If the child's grades are falling, if the child is isolating in their room, not coming out, not socializing, not playing, not doing things they used to do. If there is any change in their routine, that means you need to get help."[35] Changes in behavior can be a telling sign that a child who experienced trauma—whether the trauma was known to caring adults or not—may have PTSD.

Chapter 3

DAY-TO-DAY LIVING

Living with PTSD can be life changing. When Letty Salamanca was fifteen, she was in a car accident with her mother when their car slid on ice. Letty broke both wrists and injured her back and neck. However, she said her emotional pain was much worse than any physical injuries she sustained when the car hit a tree. "After a month of recovery at home, I returned to school. That day, I experienced my first panic attack," Letty said. "I was walking down the hallway at school, and all of a sudden my heart started racing. I instantly fell to the ground in fear. It felt like electricity was running through my body, and I was gasping for air. I yelled for help, and a group of people started to surround me. I honestly thought I was going to die."[36]

Soon Letty was having panic attacks every day. Her behavior also changed. She had once been an outgoing and friendly person, but the accident caused her to be more reserved. Her changed

Some people with PTSD experience anxiety that makes it difficult to take part in normal activities. This can make work, school, and even being with friends intolerable.

behavior caused her to lose touch with people she had once considered friends.

Letty hoped graduating from high school and starting college would be the jump start she needed to find peace again, but her PTSD became even worse once she got to college. She was far away from her family and her hometown, and it was difficult to manage her anxiety and depression. "My anxiety was so high that doing everyday things became impossible," she said. "I couldn't even do homework, and I barely got any sleep. My anxiety had me constantly on edge. I rarely ate and ended up losing a lot of weight. I had to drop two classes, and I started to go home every single weekend because I felt so alone at college. I would cry every night because I thought I wouldn't be able to make it to the end of the semester."[37]

Letty left college for a while and got the help she needed to deal with her PTSD symptoms. Then she enrolled in college again, but there were still days when her PTSD symptoms made it hard to function. "My PTSD has me constantly paranoid and scared that something bad is going to happen to me. There are some days that I'm too afraid to even walk across campus because I fear that everyone can see right through me. When I'm feeling anxious, my mind races. . . . I'm constantly on edge," she said.[38] Letty also has trouble driving or riding in cars as a result of the accident. She carries both visible scars and emotional scars from her car accident.

> "My PTSD has me constantly paranoid and scared that something bad is going to happen to me. There are some days that I'm too afraid to even walk across campus because I fear that everyone can see right through me. When I'm feeling anxious, my mind races. . . . I'm constantly on edge."[38]
>
> —Letty Salamanca, car accident survivor

Managing in the Outside World

Tahara De'Maio served in the US Army for 15 years and was deployed three times, including a tour in Iraq. Fireworks on the Fourth of July cause her to revisit war scenes from her past. "The things I saw and the things I heard, replay," said De'Maio. "Smells and sounds trigger scenes to replay." She has two daughters she would like to take to see fireworks, but instead, she spends every July 4 in her basement watching movies. It helps if she is preoccupied and cannot hear or smell the firework explosions. "I just try not to freak out," she said. "It's very hard because I can't control . . . the situation."[39]

De'Maio's experience with fireworks is not unique. For those living with PTSD, fireworks can cause intense moments of panic and fear. The sounds and smells can be a reminder of war, especially when they occur at unexpected times. Veterans and others living with PTSD and can better manage their symptoms if they have advance notice that a noise such as fireworks will take place at a given time. This helps PTSD sufferers mentally prepare for noises that might otherwise cause them distress.

"It's not that I don't want people to have fun," said Kevin Rhoades, a Marine who served two tours of duty in Iraq. "On the Fourth of July I'm going to pop my own fireworks. But when you get woken up at two, three o'clock in the morning, it brings back those memories. I just want people to have awareness of the veterans, to just be respectful because there are a lot more people who have more stress than I do."[40]

PTSD at Home

For some people living with PTSD, home is where they can find solace from their symptoms. But for others, like Emily Durant (not her real name), home was the place where her trauma began. Emily was only eight years old when her mother's behavior changed suddenly. Emily was expected to cook, clean, and manage many other chores inside their home. Her mother said if Emily told anyone about the conditions at home, she would be put in foster care and her cats would be put to sleep. Emily was beaten with a coat hanger or denied food if her chores weren't done. "Lots of nights, I couldn't fall asleep for hours,"

Emily said. "I started having panic attacks pretty frequently at school—at least one a month—and I'd have to ask to go to the restroom or nurse because I thought I was going to pass out or have a stroke or something every time."[41]

Emily struggled with the abuse and the resulting trauma for much of her childhood. Eventually she was able to tell her story and get the support she needed. "I was severely depressed, to the point of feeling suicidal at times. I had extreme general and social anxiety. Uncontrollable intrusive memories of things that have happened to me over the years would lead to me feeling even more depressed and anxious. I finally realized I needed help," Emily said.[42] At age eighteen, she moved out of her mother's house and started going to therapy to continue working through her PTSD.

Sam Black had a similar experience, having also been abused by his mother. While he is now grown, there are moments when he is reminded of what he lived through as a child. "It's not normally something big; it's the little things, a raised hand, a raised voice," he said. "Sometimes it's just people with blonde hair or with visible symptoms of illicit drug use. Sometimes the look in a

> "I was severely depressed, to the point of feeling suicidal at times. I had extreme general and social anxiety. Uncontrollable intrusive memories of things that have happened to me over the years would lead to me feeling even more depressed and anxious. I finally realized I needed help."[42]
>
> —Emily Durant (pseudonym), childhood abuse survivor

What Is a Trigger?

People with PTSD refer to incidents that spark their symptoms as triggers. A trigger is a reminder of a traumatic event, such as an assault, or a series of events, such as childhood abuse. Triggers can be associated with any of the body's five senses, so they can be something a person hears, sees, tastes, smells, or touches. In some cases, a trigger might involve a combination of the senses. A person with PTSD might be triggered when something like weather conditions or a calendar date match up with one's own traumatic event.

Syrah London lives with PTSD and identifies triggers as the reason for a flare-up of her symptoms. "The triggers [have] the power to cause anything from an [emotional] episode to intense suicidal urges," she said. "Anything from seeing something on TV to someone accidentally saying the wrong thing can cause extreme bouts of anxiety. It's come to the point where I now have to avoid certain places and settings, for fear of having an episode and embarrassing myself and the people I'm with."[1]

Some public institutions, including universities, now apply trigger warnings to instructional content that might lead someone with PTSD to have flashbacks or other symptoms. "While there's an active wound you're working on healing, it makes sense not to aggravate it," says Andrea Bonior, clinical psychologist and adjunct professor at Georgetown University. "You can use trigger warnings to avoid making the wound deeper in the interim. It's a scab healing."[2]

1. Syrah London, "My Daily Struggle: I Live with PTSD and Was Never in the Military," *Elite Daily,* October 7, 2015, www.elitedaily.com.

2. Casey Gueren and Anna Borges, "10 Things Psychologists Want You to Know about Trigger Warnings," *BuzzFeed News,* September 8, 2016. www.buzzfeed.com.

person's eye makes me cross the street to avoid them because they look like 'her' eyes and that terrifies me."[43]

When Black encounters situations that remind him of his childhood, he is taken back to those years, and it interrupts his current reality. "I feel it all: the fear, the sadness, the cold air in most memories. The tears on my cheeks. I see it play out before me, looking through my own eyes. I hear everything: the yelling, the banging, my muffled sobs as I hide from the threats being screamed at me through the door," he said. Black recognizes that even though he has gotten help and is out of his childhood situation, there are times when his PTSD makes it hard to converse with other people for fear of their reaction. "PTSD for me is being scared that a 'no,' or 'I don't want to,' will be met with anger," he said. "These days I can manage it better . . . but the second [what I want is] met with anything other than acceptance, I lose my will to fight for it. To me, a conflict avoided means another day I'm safe."[44]

Surviving PTSD

Sandra (last name withheld) started having flashbacks associated with PTSD after being sexually assaulted by an intruder in her apartment. "During something as normal as washing the dishes, I'd be taken back," she said. "My body and mind felt like I was reliving the moment it happened. Flashbacks would last a second, a minute, or longer. I had nightmares at night. It was hard to fall asleep, and I'd wake up, afraid from the nightmare. Days, I was exhausted and had no energy. The slightest noise made me jump. I wouldn't be able to breathe. My heart pounded. I couldn't make simple decisions, like what to wear."[45]

Sandra reached a breaking point when her emotional anguish felt as painful as a physical injury. She knew she needed to get help. When she talked with a therapist and shared her symptoms, he knew it was PTSD. Learning that others experienced the same symptoms she had been having was a great relief to her. "My mouth opened wide. . . . Somebody else had this. . . . There was a way to get better. I felt so much better knowing there was a name for it."[46]

Visiting a therapist who specialized in trauma helped Sandra recover. In addition to talking about her feelings and learning ways to cope, she started taking medication to ease her symptoms. "I was afraid to take medication at first. I didn't want anything that could make me numb. I wanted to be alert at all times, so I could protect myself," she said.[47] Her treatment helped to improve her close relationships, and she found a way to channel her pain by forming a nonprofit organization and speaking out about sexual assault.

P.K. Philips suffered through a childhood and adolescence marked by physical, mental, and sexual abuse, as well as an attack at knifepoint when she was an adult that made her fear for her life. "For months after the attack," she said, "I couldn't close my eyes without envisioning the face of my attacker. I suffered horrific flashbacks and nightmares. For four years after the attack I was unable to sleep alone in my house. I obsessively checked windows, doors, and locks."[48]

For some years, Philips managed her symptoms, but then she experienced yet another traumatic event that reopened old wounds. "I saw violent images every time I closed my eyes. I lost all ability

"My body and mind felt like I was reliving the moment it happened. Flashbacks would last a second, a minute, or longer. I had nightmares at night. It was hard to fall asleep, and I'd wake up, afraid from the nightmare. Days, I was exhausted and had no energy. The slightest noise made me jump. I wouldn't be able to breathe. My heart pounded. I couldn't make simple decisions, like what to wear."[45]

—Sandra, sexual assault survivor

to concentrate or even complete simple tasks," she said. "Normally social, I stopped trying to make friends or get involved in my community. I often felt disoriented, forgetting where, or who, I was. I would panic on the freeway and became unable to drive. . . . I felt as if I had completely lost my mind."[49] When she was finally diagnosed with PTSD, Philips felt a great sense of relief. Like Sandra, Philips was able to work through her trauma and no longer feels held back by her PTSD.

PTSD on the Job

When people work in dangerous jobs, they can be exposed to situations that predispose them to PTSD. Firefighters are among those who deal with life-and-death situations on a regular basis. Not only do they regularly put their own lives at risk when battling fires or responding to accidents, but they are also firsthand witnesses to horrific things happening to others.

Perry Hall is a firefighter who developed PTSD after being trapped in a burning building. He was rescued by his fellow firefighters but had first- and second-degree burns on his arms and torso. "After returning to work it seemed like everything was normal," Hall said. "I had been [a firefighter] at this time more than 16 years. I began having trouble sleeping, re-experiencing the fire and nightmares. I felt detached from everyone but my children. I was depressed, and very emotional. I had all the beginning signs of post-traumatic stress and did not realize it."[50]

Hall tried his best to suppress his feelings, including by abusing alcohol. One night, after getting pulled over for driving while intoxicated, he realized he needed help. He talked to a therapist and participated in a forty-hour outpatient program. He is committed

People with dangerous jobs such as firefighting may see traumatizing sights on a daily basis. They are at an increased risk of developing PTSD.

to speaking out about the signs associated with PTSD so other firefighters will get help when they need it.

As the medical captain with a volunteer fire and rescue team in New Mexico for more than three decades, Hersch Wilson notes the importance of having a game plan to take care of firefighters so they can continue to do their jobs well and remain emotionally healthy. "Being a firefighter . . . carries inherent risks, which we all accept as part of the vocation," he says. "But we also have a moral imperative to keep our firefighters safe from the effects of emotional trauma. The last thing we want is [to] hear about is one of our own who has quit or retired and is psychologically damaged, maybe using drugs or alcohol or thinking of suicide. I never want to have to ask myself, 'Was there anything I could have done?'"[51]

Firefighters and other first responders are not the only ones who can develop PTSD in work situations. Journalists who are reporting on traumatic events in dangerous locations are also at risk. Dean Yates is a journalist who spent time covering events in the Middle East and Southeast Asia during wartime. Even after he returned home, the feelings of danger clung to him and made it hard for him to function as he had before. "I'd feel like I was transported back to that place," he said. "And when I got stressed, I would just react very badly. I'd bang my fists on the table. I'd shout."[52]

After realizing he was having a hard time working through his experiences, Yates talked to a psychiatrist, who suggested taking walks and enjoying nature. Doing so helped him relax and let go of the trauma he experienced in his job. "It was where my mind was still. I could breathe. I could just leave all of that emotional baggage at home and just look at the trees, walk these beautiful trails and feel really, really at peace."[53]

Yates plans to keep working as a journalist now that he knows how to process his feelings and manage the psychological distress brought on by his job. Said Yates, "I think we have an obligation as journalists to talk about mental health issue[s] because I think we're uniquely equipped to communicate what it's like to live with mental illness. . . . I think we need to

> "I think we have an obligation as journalists to talk about mental health issue[s] because I think we're uniquely equipped to communicate what it's like to live with mental illness."[54]
>
> —Dean Yates, journalist

How to Cope

When people with PTSD are experiencing symptoms such as flashbacks, nightmares, and behavioral changes, they need to find ways to cope. Mayo Clinic suggests ways to cope with PTSD, which might make living with the disorder easier. An important first step is to follow a treatment plan. Treatment takes time, but it is the best way to recover from PTSD. PTSD sufferers should also commit to learning more about PTSD. Learning about the disorder can help people better understand what they are feeling and how to deal with those feelings.

Practicing self-care is an important component of recovery. This can mean eating well, sleeping, exercising, and relaxing. At the same time, people with PTSD should avoid turning to drugs or alcohol to numb their feelings. Doing so can hinder the recovery process. If symptoms such as anxiety start to take hold, people with PTSD should find healthy ways to direct their energy, such as walking, drawing, or engaging in a hobby.

Staying connected with family, friends, and other kind and caring people can help those living with PTSD feel more relaxed and comfortable. Experts advise casting an even wider safety net by participating in a support group, whether in person or online. The PTSD journey should never be traveled alone.

do what we can to raise awareness and break down the stigma that still surrounds mental illness."[54]

Lady Gaga Speaks Out

Openly addressing the issue of mental health is a major way to lessen the stigma of mental illness. Many people have the misconception that only military veterans or those still in active service are susceptible to PTSD. So it came as a surprise to many when pop singer Lady Gaga shared her own experience with PTSD after having been raped as a teenager. She chose to be open about her struggle in the interest of helping others. In a letter on her website, she writes,

There is a lot of shame attached to mental illness, but it's important that you know that there is hope and a chance for recovery. It is a daily effort for me . . . to regulate my nervous system so that I don't panic over circumstances that to many would seem like normal life situations.[55]

The rest of the letter outlines how Lady Gaga is sometimes frozen by fear and cannot handle everyday activities, such as leaving her house or being touched by a fan who only wants to greet her. She goes on to say it is important to let other PTSD victims know they are not alone. "I pledge not only to help our youth not feel ashamed of their own conditions, but also to lend support to those servicemen and women who suffer from PTSD. No one's invisible pain should go unnoticed," she writes.[56]

In the months after Lady Gaga revealed her experience with PTSD, she had a conversation with Prince William of the United Kingdom about mental health and the importance of public awareness. During that conversation, she said,

For me, waking up every day and feeling sad and going on stage is something that is very hard to describe. There is a lot of shame attached to mental illness, you feel like something's wrong with you. In my life I go, 'Oh my goodness, look at all these beautiful, wonderful things that I have, I should be so happy', but you can't help it if in the morning when you wake up you are so tired, you are so sad, you are so full of anxiety and the shakes that you can barely think. It was like saying, 'this is a part of me and that's OK'.[57]

Lady Gaga has spoken out about the challenges of living with PTSD. When celebrities engage in this kind of advocacy, it can draw more attention to important issues.

Prince William, who is trying to raise awareness of mental health in his country, encouraged others to speak about their experiences as Lady Gaga had. "It's really important to have this conversation," he said. "You won't be judged. It's so important to break open that fear and that taboo which is only going to lead to more problems down the line."[58]

Chapter 4

PTSD TREATMENT

When someone exhibits symptoms of PTSD, it is essential for that person to seek timely, appropriate treatment. After all, treatment is what is most likely to help a traumatized person deal with the symptoms and return to normal a life. When speaking at a town hall meeting during his presidency, former US president Barack Obama addressed the need to get help. "If you break your leg, you're going to go to the doctor to get that leg healed," he said. "If, as a consequence of the extraordinary stress and pain that you are witnessing, . . . something inside you feels like it's wounded, it's just like a physical injury. You've got to go get help. There's nothing weak about that. It's strong."[59]

After Trauma Happens

PTSD is not an automatic result of a traumatic event. It can be helpful for a person who has experienced a trauma to talk right away to a skilled therapist. By addressing one's thoughts and feelings early on, it may be possible to lessen the severity of any symptoms that arise later. "Keeping silent on the emotions you are going through doesn't make you stronger," says researcher Caryn Mei Hsien Chan. "In fact, it takes courage to talk to an expert. Many of the symptoms of PTSD, depression[,] or anxiety can be managed and resolved far more quickly with therapy, than waiting months or years for these symptoms to go away on their own."[60] Addressing these issues early in the recovery process can be considered a form of psychological first aid.

> "If, as a consequence of the extraordinary stress and pain that you are witnessing, . . . something inside you feels like it's wounded, it's just like a physical injury. You've got to go get help. There's nothing weak about that. It's strong."[59]
>
> —Barack Obama, former US president

Many people who have been through a traumatic experience want to resume their normal lives as soon as possible. Returning to a normal routine can be especially critical for children. "In children, the loss of their normal routine and their sense of safety is really disruptive, and it can be a very confusing time," says Melissa Allen, the medical director of the UTHealth Harris County Psychiatric Center. "So it's important to re-establish a sense of normalcy as soon as possible, and to talk with a child who has been through something like this and see what it is they need, what they [feel] happened, and just be there to reassure [them] that they are in a safe place now."[61]

Meeting with a trained therapist can be extremely beneficial for a person with PTSD. A therapist can offer a respectful, knowledgeable perspective on the disorder.

Traditional PTSD Treatments

Psychotherapy is an essential treatment for PTSD, according to the APA. The first step in beginning therapy is to find a qualified practitioner with experience in treating patients who have PTSD. Issues to consider in evaluating a provider include educational background, previous clinical experience, types of therapy employed, use of medications, and practical considerations such as office location, schedule, and fees. Since a therapist and his or her patient need to collaborate effectively as they address the patient's concerns, it is essential to select a therapist with whom one can establish a rapport. At a minimum, an effective therapist must be respectful and knowledgeable and must offer patients hope that improvement is possible.

Based on scientific evidence, the APA strongly recommends various forms of cognitive behavioral therapy (CBT). CBT is designed to address the connection between the way people think, feel, and act. To some degree, CBT means people must confront the memory of the trauma or at least discuss the trauma they lived through in order to move past it. The approach is solutions oriented, encouraging patients to examine how their thinking patterns are not serving them well. CBT is a common treatment that has proven effective for adults and children as young as three years old.

A subset of CBT that is effective with PTSD sufferers is cognitive processing therapy, or CPT. This therapy helps people identify ways they can change how they think about their trauma. For example, a person who was mugged and robbed might wonder if he had made bad judgments that put him at risk. CPT can help him stop blaming himself and accept that he was the victim of another person's wrongdoing. Once people change their thoughts about what happened to them, they can make forward progress in their life. CBT typically takes place over the course of twelve weeks, with one session per week. The sessions normally last from sixty to ninety minutes and can be conducted in a one-on-one setting with a therapist or in a group.

Prolonged exposure therapy (PE) is another type of treatment for PTSD. In PE, patients gradually face the memories and scenarios that caused them stress or fear. Doing so can lessen PTSD symptoms. With the help of a therapist, PE patients practice identifying the people, places, memories, and activities they have avoided because of their PTSD. While the duration of treatment differs from patient to patient, a typical length of treatment is approximately three months, consisting of eight to fifteen sessions lasting sixty to ninety minutes each. Patients are assigned tasks to complete at home, such as listening to a recording of themselves recounting the details of their trauma. Therapists also teach breathing techniques to help patients manage their anxiety as they work through the desensitization process.

Eye movement desensitization and reprocessing, or EMDR, is another commonly used treatment for PTSD. EMDR is a type of psychotherapy that results in people modifying the way they feel, think, and remember the traumatic event or events that led to their PTSD. This is done by making back-and-forth eye movements or responding to sounds such as tapping or tones. Focusing on the sounds employed in EMDR has been shown to make the memories less vivid, thus lowering one's emotional response. EMDR is an individual therapy that doesn't require people to talk about their trauma; nonetheless, focusing on particular elements of a memory can be uncomfortable. "Our experiments clearly show that negative autobiographical memories are very rich in sensory detail, and by pairing them with eye movements, they lose this sensory richness," said Chris Lee, a psychologist who has

> "Our experiments clearly show that negative autobiographical memories are very rich in sensory detail, and by pairing them with eye movements, they lose this sensory richness. People describe that the memories become less vivid and more distant, that they seem further in the past and harder to focus on."[62]
>
> —Chris Lee, psychologist

studied EMDR. "People describe that the memories become less vivid and more distant, that they seem further in the past and harder to focus on. What follows after this distancing is a reduction in the associated emotional levels."[62]

EMDR normally takes about ninety minutes per session and is repeated every week for four to twelve weeks. The process is completed in phases, with the first phase focused on taking an inventory of what the treatment will address. Then a therapist will ask questions about the targeted memories while the patient follows the back-and-forth movement or sound. Over the course of the treatment, someone who previously had negative feelings and thoughts about his or her traumatic memories can be transformed, gaining a more positive association for those memories.

While appropriate and timely psychotherapy is highly recommended, the first priority in treatment should be the safety and overall well-being of the patient and his or her family. "Anybody on the verge of hurting themselves or someone else does not need to be talking about the nitty gritty details of their trauma," says therapist Lori Moskel. "There needs to be basic stabilization work first."[63] Clinicians skilled in treating PTSD can assess whether a patient needs to be stabilized, perhaps in a hospital, before therapy can begin.

The other type of traditional treatment for PTSD, often used in conjunction with psychotherapy, is medication. Antidepressants used to treat anxiety and depression disorders are most commonly prescribed for PTSD. These antidepressants target brain chemicals known as neurotransmitters and serve to balance one's mood and emotions. A doctor can prescribe an antidepressant or other medication that might help symptoms of PTSD be more manageable.

Activities such as art, crafts, and music can help people recover from trauma. These hobbies can help people express their emotions in a healthy way.

Complementary Therapies

Experts in the field rely on traditional forms of treatment that have been proven to improve quality of life for those living with PTSD, but complementary therapies are also in use to help PTSD sufferers manage their symptoms. Therapies that utilize calming activities such as art, crafts, and music can be beneficial in dealing with trauma. Such methods can help people tap into their creativity and uncover issues that might be hiding under the surface. "Art expression is a powerful way to safely contain and create separation from the terrifying experience of trauma," according to board-certified art therapist Gretchen Miller. "Art safely gives voice to and makes a survivor's experience of emotions, thoughts, and memories visible when words are insufficient."[64] Joe McClain, a retired US Navy captain and CEO of an organization called Help Heal Veterans, has seen benefits with craft therapy. "Craft therapy . . . gives veterans a sense of pride, purpose and productivity, as well as opportunities to connect with family and friends," says McClain. "The sad reality is that many vets will come home with psychological wounds. Fortunately, the medical community is learning more about effective treatments every day."[65]

Music therapy has also proven effective in reducing PTSD symptoms. In a 2010–2011 study sponsored by the US Department of Veterans Affairs, forty war veterans were given a guitar, along with weekly guitar instruction, for six weeks. By the end of the study, there was measurable improvement in the participants' depression symptoms and health-related quality of life. Additional research is needed to measure the effectiveness of music therapy in treating PTSD.

Music is also a useful tool outside of the therapeutic setting, as it can stimulate the brain and distract people from their pain or other PTSD symptoms. Charles Browne developed PTSD after serving in Vietnam, and his primary symptom was being able to sleep only one hour a night. His doctor suggested he listen to music to help him sleep longer. Browne found that doing so made a huge difference. He was able to sleep as many as five hours a night after incorporating music into his nightly routine.

Aside from creative therapies, physical activity can also be used to help lower stress and minimize other PTSD symptoms. A 2014 study showed that a twelve-week running program combined with psychotherapy raised the level of brain-derived neurotrophic factor (BDNF), a protein that helps the brain repair itself. BDNF, which is also associated with the ability to learn and remember, is known to be lower than normal in PTSD sufferers. Study participants who combined regular running with talk therapy saw increases in their BDNF levels compared to participants who engaged in talk therapy alone. "It's exciting that something so straightforward—running— can have such a large impact on the treatment of PTSD," said Mark Powers, lead author of the study.[66]

Dogs Bring Healing

Animals, particularly dogs, can ease the pain of people who are living with PTSD. Emotional support and service dogs can be especially helpful to people who have sustained abuse, assault, or trauma involving another person, all of which can negatively affect victims' ability to trust others. Service dogs are specially trained to do tasks their owners cannot do because of a disability. Emotional support dogs are trained so they will behave well in public, but their primary role is to be there for their handlers emotionally. Because dogs are loyal to and protective of their owners, people with PTSD gain the comfort of having their dog care about their well-being. Dogs also help PTSD survivors be able to love and trust someone again.

Service dogs can be trained to help those with PTSD manage specific symptoms such as anxiety and fear. Veteran Mark Hansen was plagued with nightmares after serving tours of duty in Iraq and Afghanistan. His service dog, Junior, is trained to wake Hansen up when a nightmare is going on. "From the first night, he was waking

Therapy dogs are increasingly being used to aid people living with PTSD. They can comfort people and reduce anxiety.

me up from nightmares," said Hansen. Junior knows to pull on a special tab on Hansen's blanket in order to wake him up, but if the tab is not accessible or if pulling doesn't work, he nudges Hansen until Hansen wakes up. "He won't stop until I acknowledge him and tell him everything is OK. Then he knows, 'OK, I can go back to sleep,'" Hansen said.[67]

Some programs, such as Paws for Purple Hearts, give veterans with PTSD the opportunity to train a dog for another veteran, which helps them focus on something other than their own symptoms. "The training of a dog requires you to emote," says Rick Yount, founder of Paws for Purple Hearts. "That's hard for a guy with PTSD who's emotionally numb. But if you tell them it's necessary to train this dog to help a fellow vet, there's motivation. First, they have to sound happy. It's fake. . . . Within a few days, it sounds more and more sincere. Pretending to sound happy actually impacts your feeling of happiness."[68]

It can cost more than $25,000 to raise and train a service dog; the cost for training an emotional support dog is considerably less. More studies are needed to document the measurable benefits of service and emotional support dogs for PTSD victims. But people who work closely with PTSD patients believe the impact of service and emotional support dogs is life changing. "If the dog considerably improves quality of life, which is what I've seen, it's almost indescribable how much it's worth for that person," says Colonel Elspeth Cameron Ritchie, a retired US Army psychiatrist.[69]

The Future: Technology-Based Treatments

In addition to psychotherapy, medication, and complementary therapies, other options have recently come into use, though mainly in research settings. One newer type of therapy is virtual reality (VR) therapy. This emerging therapy has been gaining popularity because it can simulate the experiences people need to overcome without forcing them into real-world situations. Marine Jimmy Castellanos lived with extreme trauma upon completion of his military duty in Iraq. For years after his return, whenever he used a public bathroom, he would check behind the door of every stall to ensure his safety. Castellanos's doctors enrolled him in a research trial combining VR with a medication believed to make VR more effective.

At his first treatment session, Castellanos was handed a replica M16 rifle and a virtual reality headset. He was hooked up to monitors that tracked his heart rate and eye movements. The scenes that flashed through the headset were extraordinarily realistic, making Castellanos think he was back in Iraq. The experience was made even more intense by a puff of air being directed toward his neck when an explosion occurred on screen. "My heart was beating. I was sweating. . . . I almost freaked out."[70]

Immediately after his first session, Castellanos was asked the names of basic colors and shapes. He was unable to answer the questions. "I had completely lost all psychological control. It was absolutely bizarre."[71] But over the course of his treatment, Castellanos made great strides toward recovery.

VR is likely to grow in popularity as a treatment for various mental health disorders because it can help people learn to respond differently to something that previously terrified them. "There are very few conditions VR can't help, because, in the end, every mental health problem is about dealing with a problem in the real world, and VR can produce that troubling situation for you," says British psychology professor Daniel Freeman, an early adopter of VR.

Says Freeman,

It gives you a chance to coach people in other ways of responding. The people I see are anxious or depressed, or worried about people attacking them, and what they've done in their life is retreat from the world. With VR, you can get

> "There are very few conditions VR can't help, because, in the end, every mental health problem is about dealing with a problem in the real world, and VR can produce that troubling situation for you."[72]
>
> —Daniel Freeman, psychology professor

*people to try stuff they haven't done for years—go in [elevators],
to shopping malls, then they [realize] they can do it out in the
real world.*[72]

Technology is driving the change in therapies and treatment for PTSD at research centers. In 2016, the University of Southern California's Institute for Creative Technologies developed a virtual therapist named Ellie. Through an appointment with Ellie, patients can have an anonymous interview with a computerized avatar. Ellie can listen to what people have to say and simultaneously scan their faces for clues that allow her to respond as a real person would. Researchers observed that recently returned military veterans reported more symptoms to Ellie than they did on their post-deployment written surveys. "Getting people to admit they have symptoms is an important step in helping them realize they're at risk—and getting them treatment," says Gale Lucas, a psychologist at the institute.[73]

Another interesting twist on using technology to treat PTSD emerged from Sweden's Karolinska Institute in 2017. Researchers found intrusive memories and other symptoms of PTSD were lessened if car accident victims played the video game *Tetris* within hours of their accident. Researchers hypothesize that forcing the mind to focus on *Tetris*'s visual cues prevented the traumatic memories from being cemented in the victims' minds. "Anyone can experience trauma," said Emily Holmes, a psychology professor who led the *Tetris* study. "It would make a huge difference to a great many people if we could create simple behavioral psychological interventions using computer games to prevent post-traumatic suffering and spare them these grueling intrusive memories."[74] Technology-based treatment options

Where to Find Help

It is critical that people affected by trauma receive skilled, professional support to help them work through their issues. There is no shame in asking for help, and the sooner help is sought, the faster the recovery. Seeking treatment when symptoms first appear is better than waiting to do so during a mental health crisis.

A doctor, therapist, or other mental health professional will want to know about a patient's symptoms, any relevant experiences in a patient's past that may have contributed to those symptoms, and ways the patient's life has been impacted by the symptoms. Relevant life stresses include impaired family relationships, difficulty concentrating or remembering, and avoidance of places or activities that bring up painful memories. The health care professional or team of professionals will collaborate with the patient to design an effective treatment plan.

Numerous services are available for people in crisis situations, including the following:

- The National Suicide Prevention Lifeline is available 24 hours a day, seven days a week. Calling the Lifeline at 1-800-273-8255 is free and confidential. By pressing 1 after dialing (or texting 838255), callers who are military veterans can access a crisis phone line. There is also an option for an online chat with a counselor.

- Help for trauma survivors can be found through the Disaster Distress Helpline by calling 1-800-985-5990 or texting TalkWithUs to 66746.

- The Crisis Text Line is available 24 hours a day in the United States by texting START to 741741.

such as computerized avatars or video games are not widely available at present. Further research is needed to determine whether they hold promise for treating PTSD survivors on a larger scale.

Self-Care

Enlisting the help of other people, particularly medical professionals, will help those with PTSD better understand their symptoms and manage the outcomes of their disorder. But there are other ways

How to Help Someone with PTSD

If something traumatic happens to someone you love, it is normal to want to help the person manage what he or she is feeling. Sometimes a person with PTSD may say he or she does not want help; others may want help but don't know how to ask for it.

The National Center for PTSD has outlined ways to help those you love:

- Learn as much as you can about PTSD. Knowledge will equip you to help in the best way possible.

- Go along on doctor visits with your friend or family member. You can keep track of what the doctor says and can help alleviate anxiety that might arise.

- Be available to listen, but understand that your loved one may not feel like talking.

- Plan activities and outings your loved one is likely to enjoy. Physical exercise can be very beneficial for both of you as you manage stress.

- Work to establish a support network of family and friends so you are not the only one offering support. Take care of yourself as you take care of your loved one.

people can try to stay calm and manage their symptoms outside of defined therapies. One technique that may help people manage the stress of PTSD is being mindful and grounded. People who are grounded are more in tune with both their bodies and their thoughts, and they are better able to regulate their emotions and behavior. Ways to stay grounded include going outside and connecting with nature, walking, taking deep breaths, praying, taking a shower or washing hands, staying present in the moment, spending time with pets, touching or hugging a trusted person, and practicing aromatherapy.

Certain holistic approaches can be useful alongside traditional or emerging therapies. Strategies such as mindfulness can foster calmness and a clearer sense of self. Mindfulness involves maintaining awareness of one's thoughts, emotions, and current experiences.

Yoga is one discipline that promotes this kind of self-awareness. Many PTSD sufferers find comfort in these holistic methods. "Any time we tell someone we have a treatment for them that doesn't involve drugs or talking about their trauma, it can be compelling," says James Douglas Bremner, professor of psychiatry at Emory University.[75] Activities that focus on mindfulness can have a positive effect on both emotional well-being and physical indicators such as blood pressure and heart rate.

Other ways people try to heal from PTSD include focusing on nutrition or adding supplements to their diets, using essential oils, investing in treatments to reduce tension such as saunas and hot tubs, and receiving massage therapy or chiropractic care. With a wide range of treatment options to choose from, people with PTSD should work with an expert to discover what will work best for them.

There is no single right way to approach treatment for PTSD, and people may respond differently to the available treatment options. The most important first step for those living with the symptoms and stress of the disorder is being willing to get help. Developing a treatment plan with a doctor or mental health professional and then outlining realistic goals and priorities is key. Mental health professionals can recommend treatment plans that are supported by years of research and evidence. A well-formulated treatment approach, particularly if buttressed by strong family support, can help people work through their symptoms in a safe, gradual, and personal way. While life may never be the same as it once was, a person who is willing to work hard at recovery can be hopeful about returning to a satisfying, meaningful life.

SOURCE NOTES

INTRODUCTION: WEATHERING THE STORM OF PTSD

1. Quoted in Patti Neighmond, "Katrina's Emotional Legacy Includes Pain, Grief, and Resilience," *NPR Shots,* August 14, 2015. www.npr.org.

2. Quoted in Donovan X. Ramsey, "Recovering from PTSD after Hurricane Katrina," *The Atlantic,* September 1, 2015. www.theatlantic.com.

3. Quoted in Ramsey, "Recovering from PTSD after Hurricane Katrina."

4. Quoted in Bridgette Bjorlo, "Gatlinburg Wildfire Survivors Struggle with Post-traumatic Stress," *WKRN,* March 3, 2017. wkrn.com.

5. Quoted in Robert Rhoden, "Hurricane Harvey Could Trigger PTSD in Katrina Survivors: Coroner," *Nola.com,* August 25, 2017. www.nola.com.

6. Dani Bostick, "PTSD: It's Not Just for Veterans," *HuffPost*, October 19, 2015. www.huffingtonpost.com.

CHAPTER 1: WHAT IS PTSD?

7. Anxiety and Depression Association of America. *Posttraumatic Stress Disorder (PTSD),* n.d. https://adaa.org.

8. US Department of Veterans Affairs National Center for PTSD, *How Common is PTSD?* October 3, 2016. www.ptsd.va.gov.

9. Quoted in Kathryn Doyle, "PTSD Can Persist for Years in Kids, but Parents May Not See It," *Reuters,* November 8, 2016. www.reuters.com.

10. Quoted in Perri Klass, "Haunted by a Child's Illness," *New York Times,* October 14, 2013. well.blogs.nytimes.com.

11. National Institute of Mental Health, *Coping with Traumatic Events,* February 2017. www.nimh.nih.gov.

12. Quoted in Judith Graham, "Grief Can Become So Deep That Life Becomes Paralyzed," *Chicago Tribune,* June 4, 2015. www.chicagotribune.com.

13. US Department of Veterans Affairs National Center for PTSD, *Women, Trauma, and PTSD,* August 3, 2015. www.ptsd.va.gov.

14. Quoted in Donna Weaver, "Survivors Struggle with Emotional Aftermath of Hurricane Sandy," *The Press of Atlantic City,* October 27, 2013. www.pressofatlanticcity.com.

15. Helaina Hovitz, "I Survived 9/11 as a Child—It Took Years to Get a PTSD Diagnosis," *Self,* September 11, 2017. www.self.com.

16. NPR Books, *For Soldiers with PTSD, a Profound Daily Struggle,* June 2, 2011. www.npr.org.

17. Quoted in Abbie Fentress Swanson, "Music Helps Vets Control Symptoms of PTSD," *WQXR,* March 8, 2010. www.wqxr.org.

18. Sebastian Junger, "How PTSD Became a Problem Far Beyond the Battlefield," *Vanity Fair,* June 2015. www.vanityfair.com.

19. Quoted in Aaron Reuben, "When PTSD Is Contagious," *The Atlantic,* December 14, 2015. www.theatlantic.com.

20. Quoted in Mac McClelland, "Is PTSD Contagious?" *Mother Jones,* January/February 2013. www.motherjones.com.

21. Quoted in McClelland, "Is PTSD Contagious?"

22. US Department of Veterans Affairs National Center for PTSD, *Partners of Veterans with PTSD: Research Findings,* March 30, 2017. www.ptsd.va.gov.

CHAPTER 2: PTSD SYMPTOMS AND DIAGNOSIS

23. Quoted in Charlotte Hilton Andersen, "Why More Women Have PTSD Than Men but Fewer Are Diagnosed," *Shape,* May 10, 2017. www.shape.com.

24. C. David Moody Jr., "When I First Started Having Panic Attacks, I Thought I Had a Brain Tumor," *HuffPost,* September 19, 2014. www.huffingtonpost.com.

25. Quoted in Godlasky, "Las Vegas Survivors Have Been through Hell. And It's Not Over," *USA Today,* October 5, 2017. www.usatoday.com.

26. Quoted in Rosemary Donahue, "PTSD: The Symptoms, Treatments, and Effects of Post-Traumatic Stress Disorder," *Allure,* October 19, 2017. www.allure.com.

27. Melissa Wilson, "Living with PTSD after Bullying," *The Grass Gets Greener,* (blog), September 10, 2014. thegrassgetsgreener.com.

28. Monika Sudakov, "Having a Flashback Is Not Simply Recalling a Memory," *The Mighty,* December 9, 2016. themighty.com.

29. Quoted in Carolyn Steber, "11 Signs Someone Might Have PTSD, because It's Much More Common Than You Probably Think," *Bustle,* August 31, 2017. www.bustle.com.

30. Quoted in Korin Miller, "We Asked Trauma Therapists How to Deal with Triggering News Headlines about Sexual Assault," *Self,* October 12, 2017. www.self.com.

31. Jordan Rivkin, "After My Father's Suicide, I Fell into Despair. I Now Know It Was PTSD," *The Guardian,* September 24, 2014. www.theguardian.com.

32. Quoted in Rivkin, "After My Father's Suicide, I Fell into Despair."

33. Quoted in Bibine Barud, "Here Are Signs That You May Be Suffering from PTSD," *BuzzFeed,* October 5, 2017. www.buzzfeed.com.

34. Quoted in Joseph Cress, "PTSD: Disorder Often Rooted in Childhood Trauma," *The Sentinel,* July 3, 2017. cumberlink.com.

35. Quoted in Hernandez, "Feeling Stressed? Could It Be Storm PTSD?" *Click 2 Houston,* September 18, 2017. www.click2houston.com.

36. Letty Salamanca, "Her Story: I Suffer from Post-Traumatic Stress Disorder," *Her Campus,* April 26, 2015. www.hercampus.com.

CHAPTER 3: DAY-TO-DAY LIVING

37. Quoted in Salamanca, "Her Story."

38. Quoted in Salamanca, "Her Story."

39. Quoted in Pete Muntean. "Fireworks Can Trigger PTSD Symptoms for Some Veterans," *K5News,* July 3, 2017. www.king5.com.

40. Quoted in Corky Siemaszko, "For Military Vets with PTSD, 4th and Fireworks Can Be Nerve-Wracking," *NBC News,* July 4, 2016. www.nbcnews.com.

41. Quoted in Elizabeth Nicholas, "The Living Nightmare of Complex Post-Traumatic Stress Disorder," *Vice,* December 17, 2015. www.vice.com.

42. Quoted in Nicholas, "The Living Nightmare of Complex Post-Traumatic Stress Disorder."

43. Sam Black, "What PTSD Means for Me as Someone Who Experienced Childhood Abuse," *The Mighty,* July 15, 2017. themighty.com.

44. Black, "What PTSD Means for Me."

45. Nature Coast Surgical Specialists. *In Her Own Words: Living with Post-traumatic Stress Disorder.* 2018. naturecoastsurgical.com.

46. *In Her Own Words*.

47. *In Her Own Words*.

48. P. K. Philips, "My Story of Survival: Battling PTSD," *Anxiety and Depression Association of America,* n.d. adaa.org.

49. Philips, "My Story of Survival."

50. Perry Hall, "A First Hand Account from a Firefighter with PTSD, *FirefighterCloseCalls.com,* March 1, 2017. www.firefighterclosecalls.com.

51. Hersch Wilson, "PTSD and the Rural Volunteer Fire Department: What Is Your Game Plan?" *National Volunteer Fire Council,* June 27, 2017. www.nvfc.org.

52. PBS News Hour, *A Journalist's Story of PTSD,* December 31, 2016. www.pbs.org.

53. *A Journalist's Story of PTSD*.

54. *A Journalist's Story of PTSD*.

55. Lady Gaga, "Head Stuck in a Cycle I Look Off and I Stare: A Personal Letter from Gaga," *Born This Way Foundation,* December 6, 2016. bornthisway.foundation.

56. Gaga, "A Personal Letter from Gaga."

57. Quoted in Newsbeat, "Lady Gaga and Prince William Team Up over Mental Health," *BBC,* April 18, 2017. www.bbc.co.uk.

58. Quoted in Eun Kyung Kim, "Prince William and Lady Gaga Open Up to Each Other to Combat Taboo of Mental Health," *Today,* April 18, 2017. www.today.com.

CHAPTER 4: PTSD TREATMENT

59. Quoted in Lindsay Holmes, "President Obama's Message about PTSD Should Be Required Viewing," *HuffPost,* September 29, 2016. www.huffingtonpost.com.

60. Quoted in Katie Kosko, "PTSD Rates among Patients with Cancer Are Three Times above the General Population," *Cure,* November 28, 2017. www.curetoday.com.

61. Quoted in Kaeli Subberwal, "From the Mental Health Wreckage of Katrina Lessons to Help Harvey's Victims," *HuffPost,* September 1, 2017. www.huffingtonpost.com.

62. Quoted in Tori Rodriguez, "Can Eye Movements Treat Trauma?" *Scientific American,* January 1, 2013. www.scientificamerican.com.

63. Quoted in Joseph Cress, "PTSD: Disorder Often Rooted in Childhood Trauma," *The Sentinel,* July 3, 2017. cumberlink.com.

64. Quoted in Renee Fabian, "Healing Invisible Wounds," *Healthline,* May 23, 2017. www.healthline.com.

65. The Pyramid, *New Treatments Help Veterans with PTSD,* August 24, 2017. www.heraldextra.com.

66. Quoted in Christine Fennessy, "Running Reduces PTSD Symptoms," *Runner's World,* June 26, 2015. www.runnersworld.com.

67. Quoted in Kyung Kim, "How Service Dogs Help Veterans with PTSD Heal, Embrace Life Again," *Today,* November 9, 2016. www.today.com.

68. Quoted in Arthur Allen, "Vets with PTSD Train Dogs to Help Comrades," *Washington Post,* November 8, 2010. www.washingtonpost.com.

69 Quoted in Roni Jacobson "Service Dogs for Sexual-Assault Survivors," *The Atlantic,* November 21, 2014. www.theatlantic.com.

70. Quoted in Simon Parkin, "How Virtual Reality Is Helping Heal Soldiers with PTSD," *NBC MACH,* March 16, 2017. www.nbcnews.com.

71. Quoted in Parkin, "How Virtual Reality Is Helping Heal Soldiers with PTSD."

72. Quoted in Simon Hattenstone, "'After, I Feel Ecstatic and Emotional': Could Virtual Reality Replace Therapy?" *The Guardian,* October 7, 2017. www.theguardian.com.

73. Quoted in Robbie Gonzalez, "Virtual Therapists Help Veterans Open Up about PTSD," *Wired,* October 17, 2017. www.wired.com.

74. Quoted in Kate Samuelson, "Playing Tetris Can Reduce PTSD Symptoms, Study Says," *Time,* March 31, 2017. www.time.com.

75. Quoted in Tara Haelle, "Mindfulness-Based Stress Reduction Therapy Holds Promise for PTSD Treatment," *Psychiatry Advisor,* December 5, 2017. www.psychiatryadvisor.com.

FOR FURTHER RESEARCH

BOOKS

Carrie Fredericks, ed., *Post-Traumatic Stress Disorder*. Farmington Hills, MI: Greenhaven, 2010.

Helaina Hovitz, *After 9/11: One Girl's Journey through Darkness to a New Beginning*. New York: Skyhorse, 2017.

Libbi Palmer, *The PTSD Workbook for Teens: Simple, Effective Skills for Healing Trauma*. Oakland: Instant Help, 2012.

Susan Pease Banitt, *The Trauma Tool Kit: Healing PTSD from the Inside Out.* Wheaton, IL: Quest Books, 2012.

Mary Beth Williams and Soili Poijula, *The PTSD Workbook: Simple, Effective Techniques for Overcoming Traumatic Stress Symptoms.* Oakland: New Harbinger, 2016.

INTERNET SOURCES

Bibiñe Barud, "Here Are Signs That You May Be Suffering From PTSD," *BuzzFeed*, October 5, 2017. www.buzzfeed.com.

Caitline Dickerson, "After Hurricane, Signs of a Mental Health Crisis Haunt Puerto Rico," *The New York Times*, November 13, 2017. www.nytimes.com.

Eun Kyung Kim, "How Service Dogs Help Veterans with 'Invisible' Trauma Embrace Life Again," *TODAY.com*, November 9, 2016. www.today.com.

Simon Parkin, "How Virtual Reality Is Helping Heal Soldiers Suffering with PTSD," *NBCNews.com*, March 16, 2017. www.nbcnews.com.

WEBSITES

National Center for PTSD, US Department of Veterans Affairs

www.ptsd.va.gov

The National Center for PTSD provides detailed information on trauma and PTSD, from causes of the disorder to methods of treatment help. Resources are available to veterans and nonveterans alike.

National Suicide Prevention Lifeline, Mental Health Association of New York City

suicidepreventionlifeline.org

The National Suicide Prevention Lifeline is a resource for people who have experienced trauma and need help. The Lifeline is available 24 hours a day, 7 days a week to offer support to people who may be living with PTSD.

"Post-Traumatic Stress Disorder." National Institute of Mental Health, US Department of Health and Human Services

www.nimh.nih.gov/health/topics/post-traumatic-stress-disorder-ptsd/index.shtml

This site outlines the basics of PTSD, including signs and symptoms, risk factors, and treatments. It includes links to videos and booklets that provide further information about PTSD.

"Posttraumatic Stress Disorder (PTSD)." Anxiety and Depression Association of America

adaa.org/understanding-anxiety/posttraumatic-stress-disorder-ptsd

The Anxiety and Depression Association of America identifies ways to help people cope after a trauma. Resources include an online peer-to-peer support group, an e-newsletter, and a database of licensed mental health providers.

INDEX

IMAGE CREDITS

ABOUT THE AUTHOR

Lindsay Wyskowski is a writer and lifelong reader from Michigan. She has a master's degree in public relations and worked within the Olympic Movement for eight years. She loves to travel and experience new cultures.